AMAZING AUTISTIC STORIES OF ACHEIVEMENT AND SUCESS

AMAZING, INSPIRING, EMPOWERING, SMALL
STORIES OF ACHIEVEMENT AND SUCCESS STARRING
CHILDREN, TEENS, AND ADULTS WITH AUTISM

SERIES EDITION VOL 1

DEDICATION

My passion for children books and inspiration for writing them is my third child, Joell, he inspired me to write books for children and individuals with autism.
Dedicated to my son Joell Russell Royalty who has inspired me to follow through with writing books for children. When my son turned three, and a half years old we found out that he has autism and tongue tie. I have been working on children's books and educational videos since he was born to help with his educational learning skills. He has been by my side from the start and finish. I just want to thank him and say I 'm proud of him for being so smart and intelligent without being able to talk or express himself how he want really too.

ACKNOWEDGMENTS

Special thanks to my wife, three kids, family members,
friends, and love one's that are no longer with us on
earth. Thank you all for inspiring me to be the best I
can be. Thanks for all the support and help. Thanks
for making every day a happy day for me through this
process. Love always yours truly!

Black Royalty Success Publishing
6080 Center Drive Suite 600 unit 232
Los Angeles Ca.90045

LEWIS J CITIZEN

Paperback: ISBN :978-8294-01915-1

TOGETHER WE COULD
MAKE A CHANGE!
Spread Your Kindness

YOU ARE NOT ALONE

Chapter 1

Amazing Autistic Stories of Achievement and Success

The Power of Friendship:
An Autism Awareness Success Story

In this amazing small story shows how the power of friendship can start with a kind act, and can help change someone else's life in a positive way forever.

Star's shine bright in all forms, shapes, and sizes. In this short story of inspiration there was a young star, named Max who lived in a small town in California City. Max had autism, which made it difficult for him to make friends. He would often be left out by his classmates and he was very lonely.

One day, while walking to school, Max noticed a small group of kids playing tag. Max was curious and wanted to join in but was too shy to ask. Just then, a girl named Emma noticed Max watching and asked him if he wanted to play.

Max was embarrassed and scared at first, but Emma was so friendly and kind that he couldn't say no. Max and Emma

quickly became friends, and soon the entire group was wel-
coming Max and including him in their games.

Max was so happy to have friends who accepted him. He
started to feel more confident and soon became a leader in
the group. He even started to join in other activities with
his new friends that he hadn't tried before, like swimming
and bike-riding.

Max's new found friends taught him that everyone has
something to offer, and that everyone deserves to feel accepted and included.

Max's story is an inspiring example of what can happen
when people with autism are given a chance to show what
they can do. His story spreads the message that autism
awareness leads to success and acceptance.

The end.

Chapter 2

This next amazing story is about an urban uptown little girl from New Jersey who believes in the power of compassion and connecting with friends. This little girl named Lily, was a sweet, outgoing child who loved to play and make new friends.

One day, Lily's parents noticed that something was different about her. She was having difficulty communicating, understanding social cues, and connecting with the people around her. After visiting the doctor, they learned that Lily had autism.

At first, Lily's parents were worried and scared, but they soon learned that autism is just a different way of looking at the world. With the help of specialists, they worked to create a safe and supportive environment for Lily to thrive in.

As she grew older, Lily learned how to communicate and interact with the world around her. She developed a passion for art and music, and she loved expressing herself through those mediums.

Lily's parents also worked to educate their community about autism. They spoke at PTA meetings and even organized autism awareness walks in their city. Everywhere they went, they reminded people that autism is a unique way of thinking and shouldn't be feared or judged.

Lily's story is one of understanding and acceptance. She found a way to connect with the world around her and express her true self. With the help of her family and friends, she was able to thrive and find joy in life.

The End.

There is nothing we can't do with a little support, encouragement, dedication, and determination. In our next short story experience is a young lady named Mia. Mia, worked hard with a positive attitude to accomplish her goals.

Mia had autism, but she didn't let that discourage her she was determined to be successful in life.

Mia faced many challenges because of her autism, but her family and friends were always there to encourage and support her. Mia had difficulty with things like making friends and paying attention in class, but she was determined to succeed.

Mia worked hard and eventually she began to make progress. She worked hard in school and made sure to take the time to learn about her autism. With the help of her family and friends, she was able to learn how to manage her symptoms and build skills to help her succeed.

Mia was so proud of herself and all that she had accomplished. She started to share her story and became an advocate for autism awareness. She started a blog and

wrote articles about her journey and the importance of understanding autism.

Mia's story inspired so many people. Her work was recognized by organizations and she was asked to speak to groups about her experiences. She was even featured in a book about autism awareness success!

Mia's success story reminds us that everyone can succeed with the right support and understanding. Mia is a shining example of what can be accomplished with determination and hard work to be successful in life.

The End

Chapter 3

This small story is about being, different can make a big difference. Embracing our differences can help us achieve our goals in a major way. Keep believing in yourself, this young woman named Sarah short story has a few inspirational tips of advice to share.

Sarah was different from the other children. She had autism.

At first, Sarah was very shy and found it difficult to make friends. She preferred to be alone and avoided social interactions.

One day, Sarah's parents decided to enroll her in a special school for children with autism. At the school, Sarah was surrounded by other children who were just like her.

At first, Sarah was scared and overwhelmed, but soon she began to make friends. She found that she could relate to the other children in a way that she couldn't to the other kids at her old school.

Sarah learned that autism isn't something to be ashamed of. She was able to make friends, participate in activities, and even join the school's basketball team.

As Sarah grew older, she became more confident in herself and her abilities. She was proud to be different and to be able to do the things that her peers couldn't.

Sarah's success in school and her positive attitude inspired many of her peers. She became an advocate for autism awareness and helped other children understand and accept those with autism.

Sarah's story is an inspiring one for all children, regardless of their abilities. She showed that with determination, hard work and a positive outlook, anything is possible.

The End

Kind people are the kind of people that everyone wants to be around. There was a young man named Alex, who lives in Los Angles California who knows just what being kind to people is all about. Alex was a sweet and kindhearted boy, but he was also different from a lot of the other kids his age.

Alex was on the autism spectrum. This meant that he had trouble understanding social cues and communicating with others. He often found himself confused and overwhelmed in social situations.

One day, Alex was in the park with his family. He noticed a group of kids playing together but he felt too shy to join in. All of a sudden, a kind voice spoke up and said, Hey Alex, why don't you come play with us?

The voice belonged to an older girl named Emma. She was also on the autism spectrum and she could tell that Alex was feeling overwhelmed. Emma welcomed Alex with open arms and soon, Alex was playing and laughing with the other kids in the park.

Alex was so grateful for Emma's kindness. He realized that, even though they were both different, they could still be friends.

Alex and Emma's story is a reminder that everyone is unique and deserves to be accepted and appreciated. With a little understanding and kindness, we can all be a little more autism-aware.

The End

Chapter 4

Spreading Autism Awareness can help people understand more about people who have autism. Understanding the facts about autism can help answer questions people have about autism. In this short story a boy name Marcus from Los Angeles California wants to know more about autism awareness, so he can help spread autism awareness.

Marcus was a curious little boy who was always asking questions and trying to learn new things.

One day, Marcus was talking to his mom and asked her what autism meant. His mom took a deep breath and said, "Autism is a condition that affects how people learn, think, and interact with others. It can make it hard for them to understand certain things and even make it difficult for them to communicate."

Marcus was surprised to hear that, but he wanted to learn more about autism. His mom told him that there are many different types of autism, and that each person with autism is unique. She also said that it is important to be respectful and understanding of people who have autism.

Marcus was very interested in learning more about autism and wanted to help spread awareness and acceptance. He decided to start by talking to his friends and classmates about autism and how they can be more understanding.

Marcus also started to volunteer his time at local autism support groups and fundraisers. Soon, people in his community began to recognize his efforts and Marcus started to become a local advocate for autism awareness.

Marcus's hard work and dedication to helping spread autism awareness paid off and his community was soon much more understanding and supportive of those with autism.

The end.

The Courageous Adventures of Jay and Ava heroes in action using understanding and friendly communication to help change people lives.

Helping others, and genuinely caring about the safety and well-being of other people is how these two heroes save the day in this next short story. Engaging in acts of heroism having concerns and caring for the people around them being able to feel what those in need of help are feeling.
Jay and Ava were best friends, Jay was a bright and outgoing boy who loved to laugh and joke around, while Ava was a quiet and sensitive girl who was always more likely to listen than to talk.

One day, Jay and Ava were walking home from school when they heard a commotion coming from the playground. When they got closer, they saw a group of kids bullying a boy who was sitting alone on the swings. Jay and Ava were horrified and ran to help.

When Jay and Ava got close, they realized the boy was having a meltdown. He was yelling and crying and his face was bright red. Jay and Ava knew right away that the boy had autism.

So, Jay and Ava took the boy by the hand and walked him home. They asked him questions about what he liked to do and tried to show him kindness and understanding. As they walked, the boy started to calm down and even smiled a few times.

When they got to the boy's home, Jay and Ava said goodbye and thanked him for teaching them about autism. They also promised to be better friends to everyone, no matter how different they might be.

Jay and Ava's adventure was a success! They had shown each other that it was possible to show love and acceptance for someone who was different, and it made them stronger friends.

The End.

Chapter 5

The Adventures of Super Dave

There's super heroes all around us helping and supporting people on a daily basis who can relate to solving problems with positive solutions. This adventurous short story is about the adventures of super David from Phoenix Arizona. David was a brave and courageous little boy. He was always full of energy and loved to explore the world around him.

One day, David's parents noticed something was different about him. He was having trouble communicating, seemed uncomfortable in social situations, and was having difficulty with his motor skills. After much research, David's parents were told that he had autism.

They were initially scared, but eventually they realized that having autism was a part of who David was. They decided to get David the help he needed, and to support him in any way they could.

David was determined to overcome the challenges autism presented, and over time, he began to make tremendous progress. With the help of his parents, teachers, and therapists, David was able to learn how to communicate with others, manage his emotions, and control his motor skills.

As his parents watched him grow and learn, they could see the potential inside him, and they decided to give him a special nickname: Super Dave.

David loved his new nickname and soon began to use it to inspire himself. He embraced the idea of being a super-hero, and used the idea to motivate himself to do and learn more each day.

As Super Dave continued to grow, he began to make a name for himself. He became a leader in the autism community and a source of support for others on the autism spectrum. He was a shining example of how someone with autism can succeed and find happiness in life.

David's story is one of success, love, and autism awareness. It serves as a reminder to never give up, no matter what life throws at you.

The end.

Words are powerful, and you are in control of how you use them wisely, stay focused on your goals and the prize rewards from doing good acts.

Learning to love and to be loved. Do unto others as you want done to yourself. Treat others like you, want to be treated. Words of affection, acts of service, spending quality time, giving others support is just what these shinning stars in this next short story experience stands for. There was a family living in a small town in Houston Texas.

There was a girl named Janet and her parents, Fred and Michelle. Janet had autism, and it was hard for her to fit in with the other children at school.

One day, Janet's parents decided to start a club at school to help kids with autism become more accepted. They called it the Autism Awareness Success Love (AASL) Club.

The club members met every week to talk about their experiences and to create activities to help them understand and accept each other. They even held field trips to places like the zoo and the fish aquarium.

The club quickly became popular and other students started to join. Janet was so happy that she was making friends and that people were understanding her.

The club also helped Janet learn more about autism and how to be successful in her everyday life. With the help of her parents and the club members, Janet was able to express herself better and make more friends.

At the end of the school year, the AASL Club put on a special performance to celebrate all the progress they had made. Everyone was so proud of Janet and all the other club members.

Since then, Janet and her family have become strong advocates for autism awareness and acceptance. They continue to spread the message of success, love and understanding.

The End

"We do not need magic to transform our world. We carry all of the power we need inside ourselves already." – J. K. Rowling

"You can, you should, and if you're brave enough to start, you will." – Stephen King

"You may not control all the events that happen to you, but you can decide not to be reduced by them." – Maya Angelou

"You were put on this earth to achieve your greatest self, to live out your purpose, and to do it courageously." – Steve Maraboli

"Believe in your infinite potential. Your only limitations are those you set upon yourself." – Roy T. Bennett

All our dreams can come true, if we have the courage to pursue them." —Walt Disney

"The secret of getting ahead is getting started." —Mark Twain

Don't limit yourself. Many people limit themselves to what they think they can do. You can go as far as your mind lets you. What you believe, remember, you can achieve." —Mary Kay Ash

"You've gotta dance like there's nobody watching, love like you'll never be hurt, sing like there's nobody listening, and live like it's heaven on earth." —William W. Purkey

Magic is believing in yourself. If you can make that happen, you can make anything happen." —Johann Wolfgang Von Goethe

"If something is important enough, even if the odds are stacked against you, you should still do it." —Elon Musk

"Hold the vision, trust the process." —Unknown

"Don't be afraid to give up the good to go for the great." —John D. Rockefeller

LOVE YOURSELF, LOVE YOU! ENJOY LIFE TO THE FULLEST EXTENT

ABOUT THE AUTHOR

AUTISM

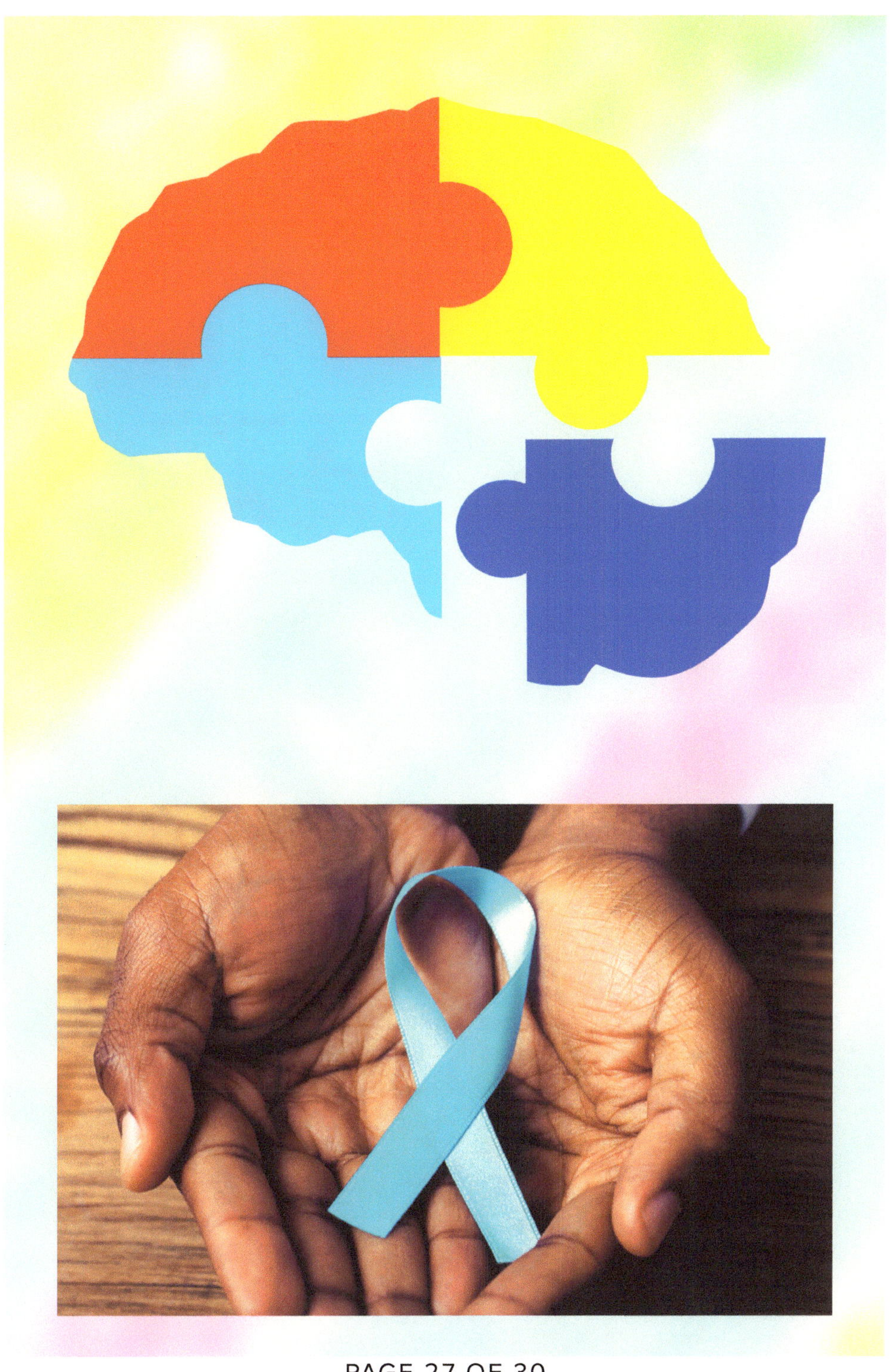

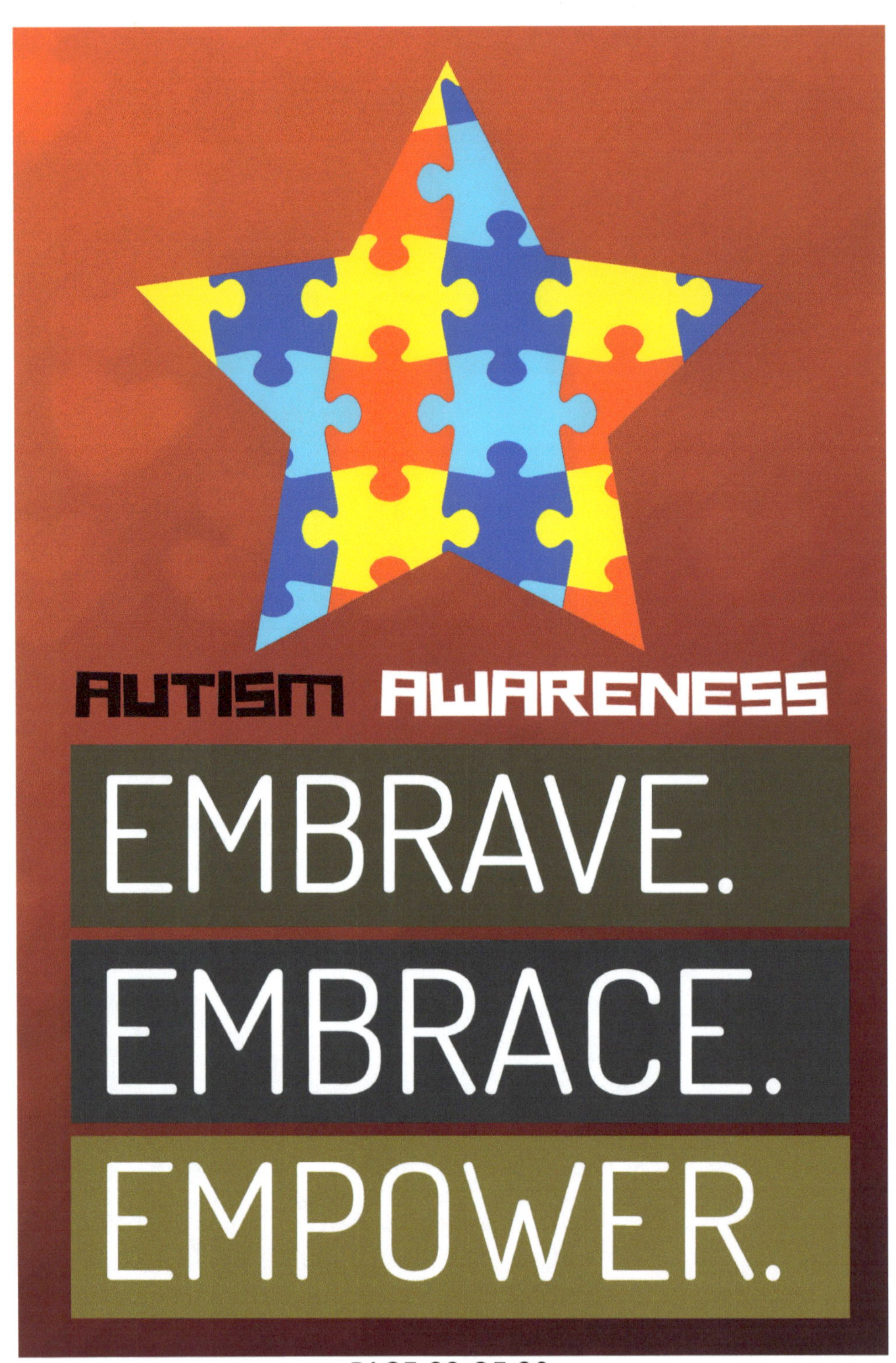
AUTISM AWARENESS
EMBRAVE.
EMBRACE.
EMPOWER.

DREAM
BIG
GOOD
JOB
SUPERSTAR

SERIES EDITION VOL1

AMAZING AUTISTIC

STORIES

OF

ACHIEVEMENT

AND

SUCCESS

AMAZING, INSPIRING, EMPOWERING, SMALL STORIES OF ACHIEVEMENT
AND SUCCESS STARRING CHILDREN, TEENS, AND ADULTS, WITH AUTISM